Last Letters from Stalingrad

Last Letters from Stalingrad

Translated by
FRANZ SCHNEIDER and CHARLES GULLANS

Introduction by
S. L. A. MARSHALL, BRIG. GEN., USAR, RTD.

Illustrations by
SZEGEDI SZUTS

GREENWOOD PRESS, PUBLISHERS
WESTPORT, CONNECTICUT

Library of Congress Cataloging-in-Publication Data

Main entry under title:

Last letters from Stalingrad.

    Translation of Letzte Briefe aus Stalingrad.
    1. Stalingrad, Battle of, 1942-1943. 2. World
War, 1939-1945—Personal narratives, German. 3. Last
letters before death. I. Schneider, Franz, 1928-
tr. II. Gullans, Charles, tr.
[D764.3.S7L4513]   940.54'82'43   73-16870
ISBN 0-8371-7240-3

Originally published in 1962 by William Morrow and Company,
New York

Reprinted with the permission of William Morrow & Co.

Reprinted in 1974 by Greenwood Press
An imprint of Greenwood Publishing Group, Inc.
88 Post Road West, Westport, Connecticut 06881

Library of Congress Catalog Card Number 73-16870
ISBN 0-8371-7240-3

Printed in the United States of America

The paper used in this book complies with the
Permanent Paper Standard issued by the National
Information Standards Organization (Z39.48-1984).

10 9 8

Last Letters from Stalingrad

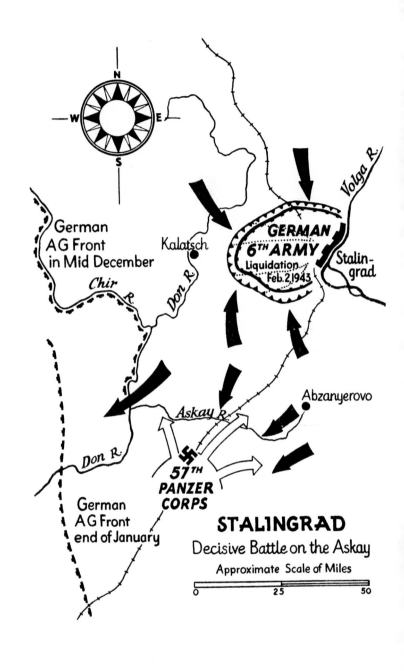

German
A G Front
in Mid December

Kalatsch

Chir. R.

Don R.

GERMAN
6TH ARMY
Liquidation
Feb. 2, 1943

Stalin-
grad

Volga R.

Abzanyerovo

Askay R.

Don R.

57TH
PANZER
CORPS

German
A G Front
end of January

STALINGRAD
Decisive Battle on the Askay
Approximate Scale of Miles

0   25   50

Introduction

What men in combat write home, though ever revealing, is rarely memorable. Yet there arises from these Stalingrad letters a dirge of melancholy unique in literature and unlike any other chorus out of battle. It is the song of the doomed, the wail of a soldiery defeated and self-marked for death. The proverbial hope which supposedly springs eternal was already fled. They knew they had been failed and fooled finally.

There is a contrast here with the Men of Bataan. Even in the Americans' darkest hour, surrender to the enemy was not preceded by universal surrender to despair. To account for the difference we must go back to the beginning of things.

The death plot from which these Germans penned their somber last messages was the same ground they had taken over six months earlier, then to relax in great dreams of an easy and conclusive victory. The first jack-booted soldier to

7

tread the banks of the Volga had no premonition that he was the advance agent of Hitler's fatal blunder, the symbol of generalship's most grievous sin—irreparable overextension. There was little or nothing in the landscape to warn him. It began as a victory march into a void. Mark the day, August 21, 1942. One panzer and one motorized division rolled unopposed to the marge of the river, taking positions above and below Stalingrad. They were but the advance guard of a mighty host. Summer heat enveloped this desert land, traversed by deep ravines which its people call balkas. But there were few Red Army soldiers about, and the German rest after the easy march made the weather seem less oppressive.

Blind confidence made them careless and the mark of their folly still interrupts the steppe. Where the spearpoint of the 3rd Motorized Division approached the river were one hill and one balka defended by a few Russians who did not come out with hands raised. It was a small thing—just a pimple on the sector—and the advance party waited for the division to come up and crush it.

The division arrived and did nothing, though there were less than four hundred Red infantrymen on the hill. The Russians were then cut off from the rest of the world, for it was much later that the underwater bridges were strung across the Volga to serve reënforcements.

Here was the epitome of the Stalingrad drama, the reason also why resistance within the built-up city wasn't crushed early when Hitler's legions were drawn up around it in overwhelming strength. It was not so much contempt for the enemy as the effect of that hypnosis which besets an army when its own field power is fully arrayed, clear to be seen, with nothing to challenge it on the horizon. Euphoria too soon takes over and normal caution is drugged.

The two-division front quickly became an armed camp, stretching for leagues. The planned blow into the blue was to be Hitler's masterpiece. Into Stalingrad ground there advanced the headquarters of five army corps and thirteen infantry, three panzer, three motorized and one antiaircraft divisions, a total of twenty composing the Sixth German Army under General von Paulus—the weightiest phalanx ever put forward by Nazi Germany. Far forward, it was still to the German eye perfectly secure, made so by its own might and the armed corridor linking it with the rear.

Stalingrad (now Volgograd) stretches more than twenty miles north and south along the river, which is more than two miles wide next the city. Weeks went by. The weather stayed pleasant. More Russians fed into the city, making the passage by night. Paulus' army, unalarmed, pawed at this local resistance, unfretted about its rear, lulled by the kind of general quiet which too often betrays soldiers.

Then Hitler began to press for stronger attacks against the city to further his prestige. In this way the formations became irretrievably committed forward, and their cream was sacrificed in bitter house-to-house fighting. In late September, Russian armored attacks from the north hit Paulus' perimeter. Bloody enough, this onfall was a fixing maneuver, aimed to hold the German feet to the fire. One German corps commander, General von Wietersheim, getting the wind up, urged that all forces along the Volga be withdrawn to the west bank of the River Don; for so doing he was relieved and disgraced. In that hour no other high German so deserved the thanks of his country.

On November 19, the first boom fell in thunderous warning. General Rokossovsky's Tank Army hit in overwhelming strength out of its bridgehead at Kremenskaya on the north turn of the Don River bend and got to Kalatsch on the south bend. There it met the other boom, another Russian army attacking northwest out of the Beketonskaya bridgehead south of Stalingrad. To make this juncture, they had collapsed two Rumanian armies covering Paulus' rear and flank. When both doors closed, his army was trapped. Thereafter, the question was whether it could be relieved by German forces to the west, or would fight its way out. No one then believed that it would be left there to perish, eating its heart away.

Hitler's megalomania forbade the first solution; and Paulus was either too weak-kneed or too stupid a commander to resist the Führer while he still had time to save his army. Their sharing of guilt, and the perversion of soul which lay behind it, is all too clear. Having promoted Paulus to field marshal thereby to buy him, Hitler then took charge of operations around Stalingrad, though he was thirteen hundred miles distant. Still, this vainglorious puppet did not turn in his soldier suit.

Cut off, too massive to be adequately supplied by air, the Sixth Army became gutted of strength as food, medicines, ammunition, arms and hope gradually ran out. But the Russian vise did not really press hard.

On December 10, 1942, the second solution was at last tried. From out of the Fourth German Panzer Army below the Don, Colonel General Hoth loosed the Fifty-Seventh Panzer Corps. Its mission was to attack eastward, cut a corridor toward the Stalingrad cauldron and thereby save Paulus and his 270,000 men. The Sixth Army was not to attack toward the corps until the corps got to within twenty miles of Paulus' lines.

There was never a vainer hope. Still thirty-

five miles short of the ground where the con-
vergence was to begin, the corps met Waterloo.
There is a small river, tributary to the Don,
named the Askay, though history has paid it
little heed. Along its banks, the last and decisive battle for Stalingrad was fought. At an
inconspicuous spot, simply called the "Railway
Gangers' Hut" on German maps, the corps was
met by superior Red Army forces and hit from
both sides, riven and wrecked.

With that, the proud Sixth Army became the
legion of the damned, though the ranks still
held to hope. Almost no information had been
given them. The further story is one of their
belated awakening to bitter truth, their physical and mental torment, the agony of the slow
march to degradation, despair and death.

On January 30, the Russians captured Paulus.
On February 3, the remnant of his once magnificent army, by then a starved shadow, ca-
pitulated. Some of its soldiers, after years as
prisoners, made it back home. Far more of them
died. Hitler's comment: "What hurts me most
personally is that I made Paulus a field marshal.
A man like that besmirches the heroism of so
many others at the last moment."

We have talked here of one of the most igno-
minious—yes, ridiculous—campaigns ever staged
by an army. So we turn now to the thoughts of
men who knew themselves betrayed.

Rare revelation, these letters bare for us the soul of the combat soldier in his worst hour. Amid the encompassing blackness, there is also a tenderness hardly less than sublime. The writers were Germans, in that hour our enemies. But who may read and not weep for them?

S. L. A. MARSHALL
Brig. Gen., USAR, Rtd.

Dherran Dhoun
Birmingham, Michigan

The letters and fragments of letters that follow were originally published in Germany in 1954 by the C. Bertelsmann Verlag (now Sigbert Mohn Verlag), Guetersloh, under the title Letzte Briefe aus Stalingrad. *The following note appeared as a postscript to the German edition:*

"A full account of the fate of these letters would make a fantastic tale of overorganization —of a military and party bureaucracy gone mad with censorship, snooping and analytical and documentary zeal. From the day they were flown out of the Stalingrad trap, the letters passed through serried ranks of bureaus. They were to be used to 'ascertain the morale of the troops'; an order was issued from Hitler's headquarters that they were to be impounded. The order went to the Army High Command and from there to the central censorship bureau of the army postal system. When, in January 1943, the last plane out of Stalingrad landed in Novo-

15

Cherkask, seven bags of mail were seized. The letters were opened; address and sender's name were removed. Then they were classified by content and general tenor, tied into neat bundles and sent to the Army High Command.

The Bureau of Army Information took care of the statistical breakdown of 'troop morale,' dividing it into five rubrics. This was the resulting 'picture':

A—Positive Attitude
  towards the Leadership 2.1%
B—Doubtful Attitude
  towards the Leadership 4.4%
C—Negative Attitude
  towards the Leadership 57.4%
D—Actively Opposed 3.4%
E—Indifferent 33.0%

After having been processed and 'taken cognizance of,' the letters, along with other Stalingrad documents such as orders from Hitler, field orders, reports and radio messages—all in all about 1100 lbs. of paper—were placed in the custody of the Army Press Corps, whose assignment it was to write a documented account of the Battle of Stalingrad. The German Supreme Command hoped to find itself exculpated, but the language of the documents was unmistakably clear. So the book was suppressed; Goebbels decided that it was 'unacceptable to the German nation.' [The German word here is 'untragbar,' which literally means 'unbearable.' In the stark simplicities of Nazi jargon and thinking it therefore meant 'exterminable.' The Jews also were 'untragbar.']

Ultimately, authenticated copies of the letters found their way into the army archives in Potsdam. From there they were removed a few days before the fall of Berlin and preserved for posterity."

1

. . . My life has changed in nothing; it is
now as it was ten years ago, blessed by the stars,
avoided by men. I had no friends, and you know
why they wanted to have nothing to do with me.
I was happy when I could sit at the telescope
and look at the sky and the world of stars, happy
as a child that is allowed to play with the stars.

You were my best friend, Monica. Yes, you
read correctly, you were. The time is too serious
for jokes. This letter will take two weeks to
reach you. By then you will already have read
in the papers what has taken place here. Don't
think too much about it, for in reality everything will have ended differently: let other
people worry about setting the record straight.
What are they to you or me? I always thought
in light-years, but I felt in seconds. Here, too, I
have much to do with the weather. There are
four of us and, if things were to continue the
way they are now, we would be content. What
we do is very simple. Our job is to measure tem-

peratures and humidity, to report on cloud ceilings and visibility. If some bureaucrat read what I write here, he would have a fit . . . violation of military security. Monica, what is our life compared to the many million years of the starry sky! On this beautiful night, Andromeda and Pegasus are right above my head. I have looked at them for a long time; I shall be very close to them soon. My peace and contentment I owe to the stars, of which you are the most beautiful to me. The stars are eternal, but the life of man is like a speck of dust in the Universe.

Around me everything is collapsing, a whole army is dying, day and night are on fire, and four men busy themselves with daily reports on temperature and cloud ceilings. I don't know much about war. No human being has died by my hand. I haven't even fired live ammunition from my pistol. But I know this much: the other side would never show such a lack of understanding for its men. I should have liked to count stars for another few decades, but nothing will ever come of it now, I suppose.

2

. . . I took out your picture once again and looked at it for a long time. I remember the experience we shared that lovely summer evening in the last year of peace, when we walked home through the blooming valley towards our house. When we found each other for the first time, only the voice of the heart spoke in us; later it was the voice of love and happiness. We talked about ourselves and about the future which lay before us like a many-colored carpet.

That gay carpet is no longer there. The summer evening is no longer there, and neither is the blooming valley. And we are no longer together. Instead of the carpet there is now an endless white field, there is no more summer, but only winter, and there is no future, at least not for me, and consequently not for you either. All this time I had a feeling which I could not explain, but today I know that it was anxiety about you. I felt, despite the distance of many thousand kilometers, that it was the same with you. When you receive this letter, listen intently to it, perhaps you will hear my voice then. They tell us that our struggle is for Germany. But there are only a few here who believe that this meaningless sacrifice could be of use to our country.

3

. . . You must get that out of your head, Margaret, and you must do it soon. I would even advise you to be ruthless about it, for your disappointment will be less. In every one of your letters I sense your desire to have me home with you soon. It isn't strange at all that you are looking forward to it. I too am waiting and longing for you passionately. That is not so much what disturbs me, but rather the unspoken desire I read between your lines to have not only the husband and lover with you again, but also the pianist. I feel that very distinctly. Is it not a strange confusion of feeling that I, who should be most unhappy, have resigned myself to my fate, and the woman who should have every reason to be thankful that I am still alive (at least so far) is quarreling with the fate that has struck me?

At times I have the suspicion that I am being silently reproached, as if it were my fault that I can play no longer. That's what you wanted to hear. And that's why you kept probing in your letters for the truth which I would have much preferred to tell you in person. Perhaps it is the will of destiny that our situation here has come to a point which permits no excuses and no way out. I do not know whether I shall have a chance to talk to you once more. So it is well that this letter should reach you, and that you know, in case I should turn up some day, that my hands are ruined and have been since the beginning of December. I lost the little finger on my left hand, but worse still is the loss of the three middle fingers of my right hand through frostbite. I can hold my drinking cup only with my thumb and little finger. I am quite helpless; only when one has lost his fingers does one notice how much they are needed for the simplest tasks. The thing I can still do best with my little finger is shoot. Yes, my hands are wrecked. I can't very well spend the rest of my life shooting, simply because I'm no good for anything else. Perhaps I could make out as a game warden? But this is gallows humor; I only write it to calm myself.

Kurt Hahnke, I think you remember him from the Conservatory in '37, played the Appassionata a week ago on a grand piano in a little side street close to Red Square. Such things don't happen every day. The grand piano was standing right in the middle of the street. The house had been blown up, but feeling sorry for the instrument, they must have got it out beforehand and put it in the street. Every passing soldier hammered away at it. I ask you, where else can you find a place with pianos in the streets? As I said, Kurt played incredibly well on January 4. He will be in the very front line soon.

Excuse me; here I am using the word "front line" instead of "first rank," [1] such is the influence of war on us. If the boy gets home, we will soon hear about him. I certainly shall never forget these hours—the kind of audience and the situation were unique. Pity that I am not a writer, so that I could describe how a hundred soldiers squatted around in their great-coats with blankets over their heads. Everywhere there was the sound of explosions, but no one let himself be disturbed. They were listening to Beethoven in Stalingrad, even if they didn't understand him. Do you feel better now that you know the full truth?

[1] The confusion is between *"vordersten Front"* and *"vordersten Reihe,"* the first of which refers to the line of combat and the second to artistic eminence.

4

. . . Just don't bother me with your well meant advice. Don't you know what kind of situation you'll get me into? The way you go on! You wouldn't have done it; you would have known how to do it! Things should have been done in such and such a way, etc., etc.! What is all that supposed to mean? You know that I am of your opinion and that we talked more about it than was safe. But you don't put that sort of thing in writing! Do you think the others are idiots?

If *I* write now, it is because I know that nothing can happen to me, and I took the precaution to leave off my name and return address; moreover, you will receive this letter in the agreed-on way. Even if anybody knew who wrote this letter, I couldn't be safer any place than in Stalingrad. It is so easy to say: Put down your weapons. Do you think the Russians will spare us? You are an intelligent man, so why don't you also demand that your friends refuse to produce ammunition and war materiel?

It is easy to give good advice; but it just won't work the way you think it will. Liberation of nations, nonsense. Nations remain the same. Their rulers change, and bystanders will keep arguing for liberating the people from their respective rulers. The time to act was in 1932; you know that very well. Also, that we let the moment go by. Ten years ago, the ballot would still have done the trick. Today, all it will cost you is your life.

5

. . . This morning in the division command post, Hannes persuaded me to write to you after all. For a whole week I have avoided writing this letter; I kept thinking that uncertainty, painful though it is, still keeps a glimmer of hope alive. I was the same way in thinking about my own fate; every night I went to sleep not knowing how the scales might tip—whether we would get help here or would be destroyed. I didn't even try to come to any final conclusion, to resolve the doubt. Perhaps from cowardice. I might have been killed three times by now, but it would always have been suddenly, without my being prepared. Now things are different; since this morning I know how things stand; and since I feel freer this way, I want you also to be free from apprehension and uncertainty.

I was shocked when I saw the map. We are entirely alone, without help from outside. Hitler has left us in the lurch. If the airfield is still in our possession, this letter may still get out.

Our position is to the north of the city. The men of my battery have some inkling of it, too, but they don't know it as clearly as I do. So this is what the end looks like. Hannes and I will not surrender; yesterday, after our infantry had retaken a position, I saw four men who had been taken prisoner by the Russians. No, we shall not go into captivity. When Stalingrad has fallen, you'll hear and read it. And then you'll know that I shall not come back.

6

. . . It is perfectly useless to rebel against it; I would most certainly find a way out if there were one. Of course, I have tried everything to escape from this trap, but there are only two ways left: to heaven or to Siberia. Waiting is the best thing, because, as I said, the other is useless. At home some people will congratulate themselves on being able to keep their chairs, both easy and academic, and in many newspapers you will find beautiful, high-sounding words in big black borders. They will always pay us due honor. Don't be taken in by this idiotic to-do. I am so furious that I could smash everything in sight, but never in my life have I been so helpless.

I continually tell myself one thing: stay healthy, and you will survive the most difficult times. Health is the prerequisite for my return home. I will not resign my chair at home. When you meet my colleagues, tell them so, exactly as I write it. The higher the chair, the harder you fall.

7

. . . You are the wife of a German officer; so you will take what I have to tell you, upright and unflinching, as upright as you stood on the station platform the day I left for the East. I am no letter-writer and my letters have never been longer than a page. Today there would be a great deal to say, but I will save it for later, i.e., six weeks if all goes well and a hundred years if it doesn't. You will have to reckon with the latter possibility. If all goes well, we shall be able to talk about it for a long time, so why should I attempt to write much now, since it comes hard to me. If things turn out badly, words won't do much good anyhow.

You know how I feel about you, Augusta. We have never talked much about our feelings. I love you very much and you love me, so you shall know the truth. It is in this letter. The truth is the knowledge that this is the grimmest of struggles in a hopeless situation. Misery, hunger, cold, renunciation, doubt, despair and horrible death. I will say no more about it. I did not talk about it during my leave either, and there's nothing about it in my letters. When we were together (and I mean through our letters as well), we were man and wife, and the war, however necessary, was an ugly accompaniment to our lives. But the truth is also the knowledge that what I wrote above is no complaint or lament but a statement of objective fact.

I cannot deny my share of personal guilt in all this. But it is in a ratio of 1 to 70 millions. The ratio is small; still, it is there. I wouldn't think of evading my responsibility; I tell myself that, by giving my life, I have paid my debt. One cannot argue about questions of honor.

Augusta, in the hour in which you must be strong, you will feel this also. Don't be bitter and do not suffer too much from my absence. I am not cowardly, only sad that I cannot give greater proof of my courage than to die for this useless, not to say criminal, cause. You know the family motto of the von H—'s: "Guilt recognized is guilt expiated."

Don't forget me too quickly.

8

. . . Again I am writing a short letter, although I wrote one to you and a second one to Hans Müllner only yesterday. You certainly can't complain about lack of mail. A buddy will take this one along. I wish Grandmother a happy 74th birthday, and I am sorry that I cannot eat a piece of her cake. Can you get the things you need to bake a cake? No cake for us, but once we are out of here, we'll have everything again; until then we simply have to tighten our belts. Go to the savings bank, take out fifty marks, and buy Grandmother a present. She is to enjoy herself. The Bergers probably have some coffee left, her husband being with the port administration. If they have some, they will certainly give it to you. You just tell them it's for the birthday party. In my time I have done the Bergers many favors.

I am writing nothing but nonsense. But nonsense is better than no mail at all. And you never know if the next bullet won't have your name on it. But don't be afraid for us. I am sure we'll get out of here, and then we'll all go home on leave for four weeks. It's very cold here now; do you have snow, too? We don't have to strew any sand here; everyone has to look out so he doesn't fall.

9

. . . Around me everything is confused, so that I don't know how to begin. Wouldn't it be better to start at the end?

Dearest Anne, you will probably be surprised to receive such a relatively funny letter. But if you take a closer look, you'll find that the letter is not funny at all. You always used to take me for a philistine, and I have to concede you a point—for example, in the way I stowed my lunch into my briefcase. One sandwich on the right, one on the left, and on top of them I put the apples, and on top of that the thermos bottle. The bottle had to lie across the apples, so that it would not melt the butter. It was a—how did Uncle Herbert always call it?—a tranquil time. Today I am not a philistine any more. You should see how I go to my "place of employment." It is cozy and warm in our bunker. We have dismantled a few trucks and rerouted the pieces to our stove. It's strictly against regulations, but that is the least of our worries.

My "place of employment" is right next door, as I already wrote you a few days ago. It too is a bunker, in which a captain lived a short while ago. Here I am telling you in great detail how things look around here, and all the time I want to write about something entirely different. Then again, I don't want to, but it is advisable and even of some importance that I do write about it. I don't want to cause you unnecessary anxiety, but things are supposed to be pretty murky here. You hear it from all sides. We are stationed a long way behind the lines; once in a while we hear a shot. If it weren't for that, we wouldn't be reminded of the war at all. As things are right now, I could stand it for another hundred years. But not without you. And it won't last that long anyway; we expect to get out of here any day. But this hope doesn't fit in with the rumors.

The army has been surrounded now for seven weeks, and it can't last another seven. My leave was already due in September, but it didn't come through. I consoled myself with the others, who also had to kiss their leaves good-bye. Yesterday morning the word was that one-third of us are going home on leave towards the end of January. The master sergeant from the staff company claims to have heard it. Or it may take a few days longer than that. Nobody really knows what is up around here. I haven't been

with you for eight months now; a few days won't make any difference. Unfortunately I won't be able to bring you much, but I'll see what I can do in Lemberg. I am looking forward to a real day on leave, and even more to seeing you and Mother again. When you receive the telegram, send news to Uncle Herbert immediately. It is good to be looking forward to something; I live on this anticipation, especially since yesterday morning. Every day I mark off a day on my calendar, and every mark means that I am a day closer to you.

10

. . . You are my witness that I never wanted to go along with it, because I was afraid of the East, in fact of war in general. I have never been a soldier, only a man in uniform. What do I get out of it? What do the others get out of it, those who went along and were not afraid? Yes, what are we getting out of it? We, who are playing the walk-on parts in this madness incarnate? What good does a hero's death do us? I have played death on the stage dozens of times, but I was only playing, and you sat out front in plush seats, and thought my acting authentic and true. It is terrible to realize how little the acting had to do with real death.

You were supposed to die heroically, inspiringly, movingly, from inner conviction and for a great cause. But what is death in reality here? Here they croak, starve to death, freeze to death —it's nothing but a biological fact like eating and drinking. They drop like flies; nobody cares and nobody buries them. Without arms or legs and without eyes, with bellies torn open, they lie around everywhere. One should make a movie of it; it would make "the most beautiful death in the world" impossible once and for all. It is a death fit for beasts; later they will ennoble it on granite friezes showing "dying warriors" with their heads or arms in bandages.

Poems, novels, and hymns will be written and sung. And in the churches they will say masses. I'll have no part of it, because I have no desire to rot in a mass grave. I have written the same thing to Professor H—. You and he will hear from me again. Don't be surprised if it takes a while, because I have decided to take my fate into my own hands.

11

. . . Today O— and I are enjoying a wonder-
fully quiet evening. For once everybody is sitting around across the street and not here. The
Russians are quiet, and we were able to close up
shop early. A good bottle of Cordon Rouge
drunk peacefully in the evening made us feel
especially good.

I read Binding's war diary and some other
things. How incredibly well this man echoes
what moves and touches us out here. He purges
the experience of all that is false and irrelevant.
Only the crucial things radiate from his mind,
from his words.

We expect nothing any more of great decisions that would have to be made . . . by the
men on top. Whether time will not outrun these
decisions anyhow, no one can say! But there is
nothing else for us to hope for. The only thing
that *has* been done until now has been fearfully
violent fighting over Hill X inside and outside
the city. Generals and colonels have played with

the possibility that this hill, of all things, might be a turning point in world history! And not only generals!

Every day a few positions are taken; every day, the enemy or we, depending on who happens to be holding them at the time, are thrown out again! Neither the enemy nor we have so far had sense enough to decide to take only what can be held.

One can safely say that with little things it is the same as with big things! This perpetual activity without result demands an indolence or an endurance which is almost impossible to muster, and since it consists only in waiting, it wears you out.

Soon it will be ten o'clock. I want to sleep as much as I still can. The more you sleep, the less you feel the hunger. And hunger is not pleasant, it's cruel.

All my love to you.

12

. . . Well, now you know that I shall never return. Break it to our parents gently. I am deeply shaken and doubt everything. I used to be strong and full of faith; now I am small and without faith. I will never know many of the things that happen here; but the little that I have taken part in is already so much that it chokes me. No one can tell me any longer that the men died with the words "Deutschland" or, "Heil Hitler" on their lips. There is plenty of dying, no question of that; but the last word is "mother" or the name of someone dear, or, just a cry for help. I have seen hundreds fall and die already, and many belonged to the Hitler Youth as I did; but all of them, if they still could speak, called for help or shouted a name which could not help them anyway.

The Führer made a firm promise to bail us out of here; they read it to us and we believed in it firmly. Even now I still believe it, because I have to believe in something. If it is not true, what else could I believe in? I would no longer need spring, summer, or anything that gives pleasure. So leave me my faith, dear Greta; all my life, at least eight years of it, I believed in the Führer and his word. It is terrible how they doubt here, and shameful to listen to what they say without being able to reply, because they have the facts on their side.

If what we were promised is not true, then Germany will be lost, for in that case no more promises can be kept. Oh, these doubts, these terrible doubts, if they could only be cleared up soon!

13

. . . Unfortunately, the Christmas I have to tell about was not beautiful, but we were comfortably warm. Our position is right on the banks of the Volga. We got hold of some rum; it was thin but tasted marvelous. My buddy brought something with him from division headquarters: ham and meat-jelly. I suppose he swiped it from the kitchen, but it tasted magnificent, and they have more, else he couldn't have swiped it. Bread is mighty scarce. So we made pancakes: flour, water, salt, and underneath it ham in the pan. The flour wasn't exactly home-grown either.[2] This is the fourth Christmas since the war started, but this time was the saddest of all. We will have to make up for it all when the war is over, and I hope that next year we can celebrate Christmas at home.

We have been in Stalingrad for three months now and still have not made any headway. It is

[2] In other words, they stole it.

rather peaceful here, but on the other side, on the steppes, they are fighting. The fellows there don't have it as good as we do. But that's their bad luck. Perhaps it will be our turn soon, because their losses are heavy. But the best thing is not to think about it. And yet you keep thinking about it; if you haven't anything to do for 24 hours but daydream, your thoughts turn towards home. Did all of you think of me on Christmas Eve? I had such a strange feeling, and it sometimes does happen that you feel it when someone thinks of you.

14

. . . The time has come for me to send you greetings once more, and to ask you to greet once more all the loved ones at home.

The Russians have broken through everywhere. Our troops, weakened by long periods of hunger without possibility of (*illegible*), engaged in the heaviest fighting since the beginning of this battle, without a day's relief, and in a state of complete physical exhaustion, have performed heroically. None of them surrenders! When bread, ammunition, gasoline and manpower give out, it is, God knows, no victory for the enemy to crush us!

We are aware that we are the victims of serious mistakes in leadership; also, the wearing down of the fortress Stalingrad will cause most severe damage to Germany and her people. But in spite of it, we still believe in a happy resurrection of our nation. True-hearted men will see to that! You will have to do a thorough job in putting all madmen, fools, and criminals out

of business. And those who will return home will sweep them away like chaff before the wind. We are Prussian officers and know what we have to do when the time comes.

In thinking over my life once more, I can look back on it with thankfulness. It has been beautiful, very beautiful. It was like climbing a ladder, and even this last rung is beautiful, a crowning of it, I might almost say a harmonious completion.

You must tell my parents that they should not be sad; they must remember me with happy hearts. No halo, please; I have never been an angel! Nor do I want to confront my God as one; I'll manage it as a soldier, with the free, proud soul of a cavalryman, as a *Herr!* I am not afraid of death; my faith gives me this beautiful independence of spirit. For this I am especially thankful.

Hand my legacy on to those who come after us: raise them to be *Herren!* [3] Severe simplicity of thought and action! No squandering of energies!

Be especially loving with my parents and so help them get over the first grief. Put up a wooden cross for me in the park cemetery, as simple and beautiful as Uncle X's.

[3] This term, which might be translated as "gentlemen," is used here in a special and emphatic sense. It means "noblemen" and beyond that, men who are their own masters.

Maintain Sch— as the family seat of the X's. That is my great wish. In my writing desk is a letter in which I recorded my wishes during my last leave.

So, once more, I turn to all of you, dear ones. My thanks once more, for everything, and hold your heads high! Keep on!

I embrace all of you!

15

. . . If there is a God, you wrote me in your last letter, then He will bring you back to me soon and healthy; you went on: a human being like you, who loves animals and flowers and does no harm to anyone, who loves and adores his wife and child, will always have God's protection.

I thank you for these words, and I always carry this letter with me in my *brustbeutel*.[4] But, dearest, if your words are weighed now and you make the existence of God dependent upon them, you will have to make a difficult and great decision. I am a religious man, you always were a believer, but this will have to change now if we accept the consequences of the conviction which we held up to now, because something has happened which has overthrown everything in which we believed. I am searching for words to tell you. Or have you guessed already? I find

[4] A small leather pouch fastened to a thong around the neck.

a rather strange tone in your last letter of December 8. Now it is the middle of January.

This will be my last letter for a long time, perhaps forever. It will be taken along by a friend who has to go to the airfield, because it is said that tomorrow the last plane will fly out of the pocket. The situation has become untenable. The Russians are within three kilometers of our last airfield, and once this is lost, not a mouse will get out, not to mention me. Of course, hundreds of thousands of others won't get out either. But it is small comfort to have shared your own destruction with others.

If there is a God. Over there on the other side many ask the same question, perhaps millions in England and France. I don't believe any longer that God can be good, for then he would not permit such great injustice. I don't believe in it any more, for he would have enlightened the minds of those people who began this war and always talked of peace and the Almighty in three languages. I don't believe in God any more, because he betrayed us. I don't believe any more, and you must see how you can come to terms with your faith.

16

. . . On the evening before the holy day, in a hut which was still fairly intact, eleven soldiers celebrated in quiet worship. It was not easy to find them in the herd of the doubting, hopeless, and disappointed. But those I found came happily and with a glad and open heart. It was a strange congregation which assembled to celebrate the birthday of the Christchild. There are many altars in the wide world, but surely none poorer than ours here. Yesterday the box still held anti-aircraft shells; today my hand spread over it the field-grey tunic of a comrade whose eyes I closed last Friday in this very room. I wrote his wife a letter of consolation. May God protect her.

I read my boys the Christmas story according to the gospel of Luke, chapter 2, verses 1-17; gave them hard black bread as the holy sacrifice and sacrament of the altar, the true body of our Lord Jesus Christ, and entreated the Lord to have pity on them and to give them grace. I did not say anything about the fifth commandment. The men sat on footstools and looked up to me from large eyes in their starved faces. They were all young, except one, who was 51. I am very happy that I was permitted to console their hearts and give them courage. When it was over, we shook each other's hands, took down addresses, and promised to look up relatives and tell them about our Christmas Eve celebration in 1942, in case one of us should return home alive.

May God hold his hands over you, dear parents, for now the evening is at hand, and we will do well to set our house in order. We will go into the evening and the night calmly, if it is the will of the Lord of the world. But we do not look into a night without end. We give our life back into the hands of God; may He be merciful when the hour has come.

17

. . . In Stalingrad, to put the question of God's existence means to deny it. I must tell you this, Father, and I feel doubly sorry for it. You have raised me, because I had no mother, and always kept God before my eyes and soul.

And I regret my words doubly, because they will be my last, and I won't be able to speak any other words afterwards which might reconcile you and make up for these.

You are a pastor, Father, and in one's last letter one says only what is true or what one believes might be true. I have searched for God in every crater, in every destroyed house, on every corner, in every friend, in my fox hole, and in the sky. God did not show Himself, even though my heart cried for Him. The houses were destroyed, the men as brave or as cowardly as myself, on earth there was hunger and murder, from the sky came bombs and fire, only God was not there. No, Father, there is no God. Again I write it and know that this is terrible and that I cannot make up for it ever. And if there should be a God, He is only with you in the hymnals and the prayers, in the pious sayings of the priests and pastors, in the ringing of the bells and the fragrance of incense, but not in Stalingrad.

18

. . . It's enough to drive me mad, dear Helmut; here I have a chance to write and I don't know to whom. A thousand poor devils who are lying in their holes up front and have no suspicion of such a chance would envy me and give me a year's pay for it. A year ago we still were sitting in Jüterbog together, cramming "military science." And now I sit right in the middle of the shit and don't know what to do with all that trash. But it is just the same with everybody else around here. It is an idiotic situation. If you should ever notice the name "Zaritza" in the OKW-report [5] (just possibly they might happen to tell the truth some day), then you'll know where I am. Do we live on the moon, or do you? We sit in the mud with 200,000 men, with nothing but Russians all around us, and are not permitted to say that we are encircled, completely and without hope.

[5] *Oberkommando der Wehrmacht,* Supreme Command of the Armed Forces.

I received your letter on Monday, today is Sunday, a real holiday. Above all, I would like to comment on the words with which you congratulated me for having been given front-line duty. I have just read "Gneisenau" (not everybody has time to do that) and would like to quote you a sentence which he wrote to Beguelin after the defense of Kolberg: ". . . On reading this news, I thought that they might have heard the thunder of our cannon and might send up prayers for our salvation. There were days when the earth shook, and I behaved like a gambler who bravely puts up his last louis d'or in the hope that his luck will turn. For there was a time once when I had ammunition for only fourteen days, and yet I could not decrease my fire for fear the enemy would become aware of my lack of ammunition. It is a scandal how badly this fortress was provided."

Ah, dear boy, those were the days. Gneisenau should have heard the rocket salvos, and the discharge of 200 guns per kilometer. Not only he, but you too, and then you wouldn't be in such a hurry to come "up front." Don't be peeved now. I don't want to shatter your faith in your own bravery, but here it would do no good. Here the brave and the cowards die in one hole without a chance of defending themselves. If just once we had had ammunition for "only" 14 days, man! would we have had fun

with the fireworks! My battery has just 26 rounds left, that's all, and there will be no more. Since you are one of the disciples of St. Barbara,[6] you can draw your own conclusions. Here I am: still in one piece, with a fairly normal pulse, a dozen cigarettes, had soup day before yesterday, liberated a canned ham today from a supply bomb (there is no more regular distribution; everyone is on his own), am squatting in a cellar, burning up furniture, 26 years old and otherwise no fool, one of those who was mighty keen on getting his bars and yelled "Heil Hitler" with the rest of you; and now it's either die like a dog or off to Siberia. That wouldn't be so bad. But to know that it is done for something utterly senseless makes me see red.

But let them come. The third still has 26 rounds and their commander an 08 with six shiny bullets. It is time to finish; "vespers" are coming, time to crawl a little deeper into the earth. Dear old boy, you can save yourself an answer to this letter, but think of my lines in, let's say, two weeks. You don't have to be clairvoyant to foresee the end. What it will actually be like, you'll never know.

[6] The patron saint of artillery.

19

. . . I just heard at the Command Post that mail is going out. I hope you can read what I am writing. There is no better paper available here. But the main thing is what is on it. And it's getting dark too. I have been detailed as a motorcycle courier and get around a lot. Otherwise I wouldn't have known that we are allowed to send letters. I am still doing pretty well; I hope the same is true of you. Except that riding around in ice and snow is no picnic. Guess who I ran into? The son of Gründel, the merchant. He is in the depot. He will be sitting pretty for a long time yet. In this way I got a can of pork and two loaves of bread. We are not allowed to send packages, otherwise I would send you the can. But then, I won't mind eating it myself either. How is little Marie doing and how are the folks? I haven't got a letter for a long time now. The last one came two weeks ago, from Richard. Now I have to finish, because it is already dark, and I still have ten kilometers to go.

20

. . . I have written to you twenty-six times from this damned city, and you answered me with seventeen letters. Now I shall write just once more and then never again. There, I said it. For a long time I thought about how I should formulate so fateful a sentence so that it would say everything and still not hurt too much.

I am saying good-bye to you, because since this morning the issue is settled. I will not comment on the military situation in my letter; it is clear-cut and completely up to the Russians. The only question is how long we will be around. It may last a few more days or just a few hours. Our whole life together is there for us to see. We have honored and loved each other, and waited for each other now for two years. It is good that so much time has passed. It has increased the anticipation of reunion, to be sure, but also in large measure helped to make us strangers. And time will have to heal the wounds of my not coming back.

In January you will be twenty-eight. That is still very young for such a good-looking woman, and I am glad that I could pay you this compliment again and again. You will miss me very much, but even so, don't withdraw from other people. Let a few months pass, but no more. Gertrud and Claus need a father. Don't forget that you must live for the children, and don't make too much fuss about their father. Children forget quickly, especially at that age. Take a good look at the man of your choice, take note of his eyes and the pressure of his handshake, as was the case with us, and you won't go wrong. But above all, raise the children to be upright human beings who can carry their heads high and look everybody straight in the eye. I am writing these lines with a heavy heart. You wouldn't believe me if I said that it was easy, but don't be worried, I am not afraid of what is coming. Keep telling yourself, and the children also when they have grown older, that their father never was a coward, and that they must never be cowards either.

21

. . . This terrible confusion has been going on for eleven days now. Today I can send you a few lines just once more. I hope that you received all the rest in good condition. I have been spared nothing either. But still, all in all life was beautiful once, so these days have to be endured calmly.

We have been pushed entirely into the city. This damned city! If only the end would come soon! Then, as I wrote before: "Let me go on my way contentedly. . . ." [7]

Farewell!

[7] A line from a hymn, so the meaning is resignation to the will of God.

22

. . . Dearest, I think of you all the time. Today, standing in the chow line I thought of you
again. Of the wonderful food you used to cook.
My socks are in shreds, too, and I can't get rid
of my cough any more. No pills are available
for it. You could send me cough syrup, but don't
use any glass bottles. Have you caught cold too?
Always put on something good and warm. Do
you have enough coal? Just go and see A—, he
got lumber from me for his furniture. Let him
give you coal for it now. I hope Uncle Paul has
nailed the weather stripping to your windows;
otherwise it will be too late for it this year. I did
not celebrate Christmas here. I was on the road
with the car, and we got stuck in the snow because we went the wrong way. But we soon got
out again. I have decided that next year we will
celebrate a real Christmas, and I am going to
give you a beautiful present.

It is not my fault that I can't give it to you
now. The Russians are all around us, and we

won't get out again until Hitler gets us out. But you must not tell that to anyone. It is supposed to be a surprise.

23

. . . We have had to swallow a lot; will swallow this too! Stupid situation. You might say, devilishly difficult. Beats me how we are to get out of here. Not really my business, though. We marched in here on orders, shoot on orders, starve on orders, die on orders, and will march out again, all on orders. Could have marched out a long time ago, except the grand strategists haven't come to an agreement yet. Soon it will be too late, if it isn't already. One thing is sure, we'll march once again on orders. In all probability in the direction originally planned, but without weapons and under a different command.

Kemner of the heavies right next to us has been shooting craps with Helms . . . Pay gone, watch, ring and an IOU, even his piano in home sweet home. Around here people get the most idiotic ideas. Am curious about the legal title to that gambled-away piano. Little Fatso won back his watch and ring. Perhaps he will win the summer-house tomorrow. But if both kick off, how will the estates be probated? Would have liked to know all that, but there won't be any time. Am ignorant of many things, will probably get over that too. As I said at the beginning, we've had to swallow a lot. Tell it to Egon. Title: "Troubles of a Second Lieutenant in Stalingrad." When the chips are down—seems to me that will be soon—we'll be in there shooting. Shoot guns even better than craps.

24

. . . Now that I know where I stand, I release you from your vow. This has not been easy for me to do, but the differences between us were too great. I looked for a wife with a generous heart, but it wasn't supposed to be that generous. I have written to Mother already and told her what she has to know. Please spare me the trouble of naming the witnesses and mentioning the circumstances which gave me proof of your infidelity. I feel no hatred for you; rather I advise you to choose good grounds for divorce and speed up the procedure. I have written to Dr. F— that I agree to a divorce. And if I am back home six months from now, I do not wish to be reminded of you by anything.

I shall pass up my leave in February or March.

25

. . . Just now the master sergeant told me that
I cannot go home for Christmas. I told him that
he has to keep his promise, and he sent me to
the captain. The captain told me that others had
wanted to go on leave for Christmas too, and
that they too had promised it to their relatives
without being able to keep the promise. And so
it wasn't his fault that we couldn't go. We
should be glad that we were still alive, the captain said, and the long trip wouldn't be good in
the cold winter anyhow.

Dear Maria, you must not be angry now because I cannot come on leave. I often think of
our house and our little Luise. I wonder if she
can laugh already. Do you have a beautiful
Christmas tree? We are supposed to get one also,
if we don't move into other quarters. But I
don't want to write too much about things here,
otherwise you'll cry. I'll enclose a picture; I
have a beard in it; it is already three months
old and was taken in Kharkov by a friend. A lot

of rumors are going around here, but I can't figure them out. Sometimes I am afraid we will not see each other again. Heiner from Krefeld told me that a man must not write this; it only frightens his relatives. But what if it's true!

Maria, dear Maria, I have only been beating around the bush. The master sergeant said that this would be the last mail because no more planes are leaving. I can't bring myself to lie. And now, nothing will probably ever come of my leave. If I could only see you just once more; how awful that is! When you light the candles, think of your father in Stalingrad.

26

. . . I still must tell you that we went to the
movies on Thursday. It was not a regular show,
otherwise you might think that we have more
time than we know what to do with. We saw
"Geier-Walli," all sat on the floor on their hel-
mets or squatting like Negroes. It is a very nice
film. You wrote me that I should be careful with
girls. But, Maria, there aren't any girls around
here. We were all by ourselves, close to two hundred men. The movie came from the propaganda
company. They play in the barn every evening;
only yesterday, so I have heard, the Russians
fired into the village. I had planned to see
"Geier-Walli" earlier in Dresden and Hanover;
but I couldn't make it then. In Stalingrad I
finally succeeded and saw "Geier-Walli." What
a joke. If I go on leave, I am going to see "Geier-
Walli" in a real movie house. I hope they will
play the film in Dresden. Even in the barn the
film was quite beautiful. Only the sound
couldn't be heard properly, and then the others

made so many jokes, and smoked so much, you couldn't see anything for smoke. Some also used the show to get warm and to get some sleep. "Geier-Walli" in Stalingrad. I'll never forget it.

27

. . . What a misfortune that there had to be a war! The beautiful villages fell victim to it and were destroyed. And the fields are not tilled anywhere. And the worst is that so many people have died. Now they lie buried in enemy country. What a great misfortune this is! But you should be glad that the war is in a country far away and not in our beloved German homeland. It must not ever come there and increase the misery! You must be real thankful for that and thank the Lord on your knees. We are standing here on the banks of the Volga and keep watch. For you and our home. If we did not stand here, the Russians would break through and demolish everything. They are very violent and many millions strong. They are not bothered by the cold. But we are terribly cold.

I am lying in a hole dug in the snow, and it's only in the evening that I can slip into a cellar for a few hours. You wouldn't believe how good that is. We are on guard, so you don't need to be afraid. But we are getting fewer and fewer all the time, and if things continue this way, soon there won't be anyone here. But Germany has many more soldiers, and they will all fight for their country. We all wish that there will be peace soon and that we shall be victorious. That is the main thing. Keep your fingers crossed!

28

. . . Even for me this letter is difficult, how much more difficult will it be for you! Unfortunately, there won't be any good news in this letter. And it hasn't been improved by my waiting ten days either. The situation has now become so bad we fear we'll soon be completely cut off from the outside. Just now we were assured that this mail will definitely get out. If I knew that there would be another opportunity, I would wait still longer. But that is just what I don't know; so, for better or for worse, I have to come out with it. For me the war is over.

I am in the field hospital in Gumrak, waiting to be transported home by plane. Although I am waiting with great longing, the date is always changed. *That* I will be coming home is a great joy for me and for you, my dear. But the condition in which I'll get home won't be any joy to you. I am in complete despair when I think of lying before you as a cripple. But you must know sometime that my legs were shot off.

I'll be quite honest in writing about it. The right leg is totally shattered and amputated below the knee. The left one is amputated in the thigh. The doctor thinks that with prosthesis I should be able to get around like a healthy man. The doctor is a good man and means well. I hope he is right. Now you know before you see me. Dear Elise, if I only knew what you are thinking. I have time all day long to think of nothing but that. Often my thoughts are with you. Sometimes I have also wished that I were dead, but that is a serious sin and one must not say such a thing.

Over eighty men are lying in this tent; but outside there are countless men. Through the tent you can hear their screaming and moaning, and no one can help them. Next to me lies a sergeant from Bromberg, shot through the groin. The doctor told him he would be returned home soon. But to the medic he said, "He won't last until evening. Let him lie there until then." The doctor is such a good man. On the other side, right next to me against the wall, lies a soldier from Breslau who has lost an arm and his nose, and he told me that he wouldn't need any more handkerchiefs. When I asked him what he would do if he had to cry, he answered me, "No one here, you and me included, will have a chance to cry any more. Soon others will be crying over us."

29

. . . Axel is writing this letter for me. His real
name isn't Axel at all but Lachmann, and he
comes from Königsberg. But we call him Axel.
My arm is propped up and wrapped in thick
bandages, so I cannot write. I'll soon be home,
the doctor told me, and I am looking forward to
it very much. There is a little piece missing on
my arm, the doctor said that too. Only the funny
thing is that I cannot move my fingers. As a
gardener I need my fingers. The soil here is
very rich and soft. We sure could use some of
that in Lüneburg.[8] There is snow outside, you
can't see the soil. Four days ago I lay in a hole
a yard deep, and all day long I observed the soil;
good soil for wheat, naturally there was no
trace of fertilizer; the steppes produce their
own. In this hole I got scared. Today I laugh
about it. I don't have a very comfortable bed,
but once I am home I'll laugh even more. And
all of you will laugh with me.

[8] The country around Lüneburg has very poor, sandy soil.

30

. . . I have received your answer. You will hardly expect thanks for it. This letter will be short. I should have known better when I asked you to help me. You always were and you remain forever "righteous." This wasn't unknown to either Mama or me. But we could hardly expect that you would sacrifice your son to "righteousness." I asked you to get me out of here because this strategic nonsense isn't worth biting the dust for. It would have been easy for you to put in a word for me, and the appropriate order would have reached me. But you don't understand the situation. Very well, Father.

This letter will not only be short, but also the last one I write you. I won't have any more opportunities to write to you, even if I wanted to. It is also unimaginable that I should ever stand face to face with you again and have to tell you what I think. And because neither I in person nor another letter will ever speak to you again, I will once more recall to you your

words of December 26: "You became a soldier voluntarily; it was easy to stand under the flag in peacetime, but difficult to hold it high during the war. You will be faithful to this flag and be victorious with it." These words were much clearer than the position you have taken during the last few years. You will have to remember them, because the time is coming when every German with any sense will curse the madness of this war. And you will see how empty are those words about the flag with which I was supposed to be victorious.

There is no victory, Herr General; there are only flags and men that fall, and in the end there will be neither flags nor men. Stalingrad is not a military necessity but a political gamble. And your [9] son is not participating in this experiment, Herr General! You blocked his way to life; he will choose the second way, which also leads to life, but in an opposite direction and on the other side of the front. Think of your words, and I hope that, when the whole show collapses, you will remember the flag and stand by it.

[9] From this point to the end, he uses the formal mode of address in speaking to the man who was his father but who has now become a mere general.

31

. . . How many letters have I written up to now? Thirty-eight according to my calculation, today's included. In August you wrote me that you keep a mail book, a real file of pen pals with their addresses and peculiarities, the dates you became acquainted with them, and how the friendships fared. It amused me greatly. Did you add the picture which I sent you to your file? My mail book is too inaccurate; your book-keeping is probably better than the little marks I make in my pocket calendar. After all it doesn't really matter whether I wrote you 36 or 37 letters. I am number five among your pen pals. It must be very interesting to read all the letters you have received. They come from all theatres of the war, don't they? When the war is over, you will have a magnificent volume of memoirs in letter form. This year, at Christmas, we wanted to meet each other for the first time in Karlsruhe. Nothing came of it. The future also looks bleak to me, very bleak. I see almost no hope.

Thank God, I have gotten around to saying it. There won't be any meeting; even the date for the coming year can't be kept. Dear girl, what a fizzle! The stupid thing is that all one can do is look on; that's what's slowly driving me crazy. If only I had toddled off for home in September, when I caught that shrapnel in my arm. But I wanted to be around when we captured Stalingrad, and I have often regretted this crazy idea since.

They were pretty funny letters you received from me; I have always been a joker, as you can testify. But jokes won't help us along now; things are getting serious.

What will you write down in column six of your mail book? In any case, don't write "He died for Greater Germany," etc., for that wouldn't be true. Write "for Hanna on such and such a date," for all I care. I hope you won't find this tone frivolous. I mentioned your other pen pals. One of these days, a few of them will go out of commission too. But their circumstances are different. They will just stop writing all of a sudden. Their letters will just stop coming. But I give you formal notice. Fräulein Hanna, this is more or less my last letter, as it were. Farewell. The hope of seeing each other some day is being sacrificed to this idiotic and totally one-sided struggle. Farewell, and as a good-bye my thanks for the time which you have lovingly devoted to me. At first I meant to write "wasted," but I thought better of it. It was not a waste of time, I got a great deal of pleasure from your letters.

32

. . . Today I talked to Hermann. He is south
of the front, a few hundred yards from me. Not
much is left of his regiment. But the son of
baker B— is still with him. Hermann still had
the letter in which you told us of Father's and
Mother's death. I talked to him once more, for
I am the elder brother, and I tried to console
him, though I too am at the end of my rope. It
is good that Father and Mother will not know
that Hermann and I will never come home
again. It is terribly hard that you will have to
carry the burden of four dead people through
your future life.

I wanted to be a theologian, Father wanted to
have a house, and Hermann wanted to build
fountains. Nothing worked out that way. You
know yourself what the outlook is at home, and
we know only too well what it is here. No, those
things we planned certainly did not turn out
the way we imagined. Our parents are buried
under the ruins of their house, and we, though

it may sound harsh, are buried with a few hundred or so men in a ravine in the southern part of the pocket. Soon these ravines will be full of snow.

33

. . . When I come to think about it, it was only here that I began to reflect on my environment, but without any positive results. One should reflect often, but it takes time. Basically, this would not be too bad, for I never had so much time as in this war, and especially here in Stalingrad. A few days ago I talked to the chaplain, and we had a long conversation together. But we did not really agree with each other, for it seemed to me that suffering is greater than the possibility of assuaging it. The chaplain thought that there we had reached a point where philosophy has to end and religion begin. One of us is surely right. But I ask myself: what difference does it make? I am continually thinking; I brood and sit in my bunker for hours.

Most esteemed Herr Geheimrat! We have no need to discuss private matters, and I am very glad not to be involved in family ties like my comrades. Those surely must be terrible and torturing thoughts, which could drive a man to despair. Those perpetual anxieties about wife and child and what not. Every day I hear what they are talking about; sometimes it is tragic, sometimes ridiculous to see how seriously they take everything, most of all themselves. Some talk about their business and wonder if their houses are damaged, others are full of worries about their packages on the way to and from home. And I pondered what those packages leaving Stalingrad could possibly contain. A fellow from Lüdenscheid who is stationed with me asks in every letter about his cat! Grotesque! Money, job, position, property. But above all the fear about their personal fate. And they write about this fear in many of their letters. I feel disgusted when I see how they behave.

Just an hour ago, a captain who shares the bunker with me asked if I had heard of the Russian breakthrough in the north. As if that could change the situation. Everywhere they are pulling together towards the center of the pocket, but the haste with which they do so raises the suspicion that they are looking for a way out. But there is no way out that they would find acceptable. Their thinking and their common sense, insofar as they have any, is destroyed by fear. And they don't even notice how ridiculous and unmanly their behavior is.

My field of vision extends only about a hundred yards and covers approximately a hundred

men. They are all alike; namely, cowardly. Once in a while someone comes slithering down the hill or limping from the front line. And starts shaking his head in wonder when he sticks his nose in here. With these people here we cannot win a war, let alone this war. It's lucky that the men on the line behave differently from this pitiful bunch of left-over staffs with their confusion of functions. I ask myself what kind of role I ought to be playing. Am I brave, or whatever one is to call it? Am I brave because I don't run back and forth from shelter to shelter, cackling like a scared chicken? Am I brave because I don't hunt for rumors and spread them, because I sleep well at night and don't make speeches about what I'll be doing on this or that day?

Herr Geheimrat! Stalingrad is a great education for the German people; too bad that those who are getting this object lesson will hardly be able to make use of it later. One should preserve the results. I am a fatalist. My personal needs are so small that the moment the first Russian comes in here I can pick up my bag and start walking. I won't shoot; why should I? Just to kill one or two people I don't know? I shall not even shoot myself, why should I? Would it be doing a service to anyone, perhaps Herr Hitler? I have learned more during my four months of war here than I could have learned in a lifetime, even if I lived to be a hundred. The only thing I regret is that I am compelled by circumstance to spend my last days in such wretched company.

34

. . . Nobody knows what will happen to us now, but I think this is the end. Those are hard words, but you must understand them the way they are meant. Times are different now from the day when I said good-bye and became a soldier. Then we still lived in an atmosphere which was nourished by a thousand hopes and expectations of everything turning out well in the end. But even then we were hiding a paralyzing fear beneath the words of farewell which were to console us for our two months of happiness as man and wife. I still remember one of your letters in which you wrote that you just wanted to bury your face in your hands in order to forget. And I told you then that all this had to be and that the nights in the East were much darker and more difficult than those at home.

The dark nights of the East have remained, and they have turned much darker than I had ever anticipated. In such nights one often listens for the deeper meaning of life. And sometimes there is an answer. Now space and time stand between us; and I am about to step over the threshold which will separate us eternally from our own little world and lead into that greater one which is more dangerous, yes, even devastating. If I could have made it through this war safely, I would have understood for the first time what it means to be man and wife in its true and deepest sense. I also know it now—now that these last lines are going to you.

35

. . . During the last few nights I have wept so much that it seems unbearable even to myself. I saw one of my fellow soldiers weep also, but for a different reason. He was weeping for the tanks he lost; they were his whole pride. And though I don't understand my own weakness, I do understand how a man can mourn dead war materiel. I am a soldier and I am prepared to believe that tanks are not inanimate materiel to him. But everything considered, the remarkable fact is that two men weep at all. I was always susceptible to tears. A moving experience or a noble action made me weep. It could happen in the movie theater, when I read a book, or saw an animal suffer. I cut myself off from external circumstances and immersed myself in what I saw and felt. But the loss of material goods never bothered me. Therefore, I would have been incapable of weeping about tanks which, when they ran out of gas, were used in the open steppes as artillery and thus easily shot to bits.

But seeing a fine man, a brave, tough and un-
yielding soldier cry like a child over them—that
did make my tears flow in the night.

On Tuesday I knocked out two T-34s with
my mobile anti-tank gun. Curiosity had lured
them behind our lines. It was grand and impres-
sive. Afterwards I drove past the smoking remains. From a hatch there hung a body, head
down, his feet caught, and his legs burning up
to his knees. The body was alive, the mouth
moaning. He must have suffered terrible pain.
And there was no possibility of freeing him.
Even if there had been, he would have died after
a few hours of torture. I shot him, and as I did
it, the tears ran down my cheeks. Now I have
been crying for three nights about a dead Russian tank driver, whose murderer I am. The
crosses of Gumrak shake me and so do many
other things which my comrades close their eyes
to and set their jaws against. I am afraid I'll
never be able to sleep quietly, assuming that
I shall ever come back to you, dear ones. My
life is a terrible contradiction, a psychological
monstrosity.

I have now taken over a heavy anti-tank gun
and organized eight men, four Russians among
them. The nine of us drag the cannon from one
place to another. Every time we change position,
a burning tank remains on the field. The number has grown to eight already, and we intend

to make it a dozen. However, I have only three rounds left, and shooting tanks is not like playing billiards. But during the night I cry without control, like a child. What will all this lead to?

36

. . . A year ago, your letter came to a stranger who was alone in this world. I picked it up, and during the long winter days I listened to the heartbeat which spoke to me in it: the heartbeat of the farmers and animals, the plants and the mountain tops, the thunder of the spring storm and the avalanches.

You always wrote that your letters were meant to give the "unknown soldier" stimulation, strength, courage and faith. Today, I have to tell you that I did draw stimulation, strength and even courage from them. But faith—faith in the good cause—is dead, as dead as I, together with a hundred thousand others, will be a month from now.

I am writing you today for two reasons. First, because according to military custom, the unknown soldier to whom you wrote a year ago has to give notice of his departure, which I now do. And second, because I assume that you will now begin to write to a new stranger, so as to give

him strength, stimulation, and courage. And faith.

Miss Adi, this is the most important reason. One can perhaps show faith on paper, but if it is, as here in this devastated city on the Volga, put on sale and hawked around; if one realizes as one does here, that one's faith in the good cause was time needlessly wasted, then one is bound to warn everybody against persuading another to this faith!

37

. . . They told us this morning that we could write. Just once more, I say, for I know definitely that it will be the last time. You know that I always wrote to two people, two women, to the "other one" and you. And to you most infrequently. I have been very distant from you; Carola was closer to me than you during those last years. We don't want to go over how it happened and why it had to turn out that way. Today, however, when fate gives me the choice of writing to one person only, my letter goes to you, who have been my wife for six years.

It will do you good to learn that the last letter of the man whom you loved is directed to you. I simply could not manage to write Carola and ask her to give you my regards. So I am asking you, dear Erna, in this hour which contains my last wish: be generous and forgive the wrong I have done you in life. Go to her (she lives with her parents) and tell her that I owe her a great deal, and that I greet her through you, my wife.

Tell her that she meant a lot to me during these last days, and that I often thought about what would happen after my return home. But tell her also that you were more to me and that, although I am very sad not to be returning home, in a way I am glad to be compelled to take this road, since it will save the three of us ghastly tortures.

Is God greater than fate? I am perfectly composed, but you don't know how difficult it is to say in one hour everything that still needs saying. There is such a vast deal still to be written, but because it is so much, one must know when to stop, take pen from paper and put it away. Just as I now put my life away.

Of my company, only five men are still around. Wilmsen among them. The others are all . . . all grown too tired. Isn't that a nice euphemism for the horror? But what is the point of talking about that now, and what good would it do you to know about it? So keep me alive in your memory as the man who recalled only at the very end that he is your husband and who asks your forgiveness; more, asks you to tell everyone you know, Carola included, that I found my way back to you at the moment which will take you away from me forever.

38

. . . I wanted to write you a long letter, but my thoughts constantly disintegrate like houses which collapse under shellfire. I still have ten hours, then this letter has to be turned in. Ten hours is a long time for people who are waiting, but short for those in love. I am not nervous at all. Actually, it is here in the East that I have for the first time become really healthy; I don't have colds and sniffles any more; that is the only good the war has done me. It gave me something else, the realization that I love you. It is strange that people value things only when they are about to lose them. The vast distance is spanned by the bridge from heart to heart. By that bridge I wrote you about our daily round and the world in which we live here. I meant to tell you the truth when I returned, and then we would never have talked about the war again. Now you will learn the truth beforehand, the last truth. Now I can write no more.

As long as there are shores, there will always

be bridges. We should have the courage to walk on them. One bridge leads to you, the other to eternity; at the very end they are the same for me.

Tomorrow I shall set foot on the last bridge. That is the literary way of saying "death," but as you know, I always liked to express things figuratively, because I took pleasure in words and sounds. Give me your hand, so that crossing it won't be so hard.

39

. . . Dearest Father, the division has been trimmed down for the big battle, but the big battle won't take place. You will be surprised that I write to you and in care of your office. But what I have to say in this letter can only be said among men. You will transmit it to Mother in your own way. The word is out that we can write today. For one familiar with the situation that means that we can do it just once more.

You are a colonel, my dear Father, and a member of the general staff. So you know what this means, and I needn't go into explanations which might sound sentimental. This is the end. It will last perhaps another week, I think, then the game's up. I do not want to look for reasons which one could marshal for or against our situation. The reasons are now altogether unimportant and pointless. But if I am to say anything about them, it is this: Do not look to us for an explanation of the situation, but to yourselves and to the man [10] who is responsible for

[10] Hitler.

it. Don't knuckle under—you, Father, and all those who think like you. Be on guard, so that a greater disaster does not overtake our country. The hell on the Volga should be a warning to you. I beg you, don't brush off this experience.

And now a remark about the present. Of the whole division only 69 men are still in fighting condition. Bleyer is still alive, and so is Hartlieb. Little Degen lost both his arms; he will probably be in Germany soon. It is also the end for him. Ask him for any details you would like to know. D— has lost all hope. I would like to know what he is thinking at times of the situation and its consequences. We still have two machine guns and 400 rounds of ammunition. One mortar and ten shells. Besides that, only hunger and fatigue. Without waiting for orders, Berg broke out with twenty men. Better to know in three days how things will end, than in three weeks. Can't blame him.

And now to personal matters. You can be sure that everything will end decently. It is a little early at thirty, I know. No sentiments. Handshake for Lydia and Helene. Kiss for Mother (be careful, old man, think of her heart trouble), kiss for Gerda, regards to all the rest. Hand to helmet, Father. First Lieutenant—respectfully gives notice of departure.

ISBN 0-8371-7240-3

9 780837 172408

HARDCOVER BAR CODE